I0476980

Leadership LIFT

Take Your Leadership To New Heights

by
Paul LaRue

Creator of The Upwards Leader

Leadership LIFT:
Take Your Leadership To New Heights

Published by Paul LaRue
ISBN-13: 978-1514349649

Printed in the United States of America
First Edition

Leadership LIFT:

Take Your Leadership To New Heights

Acknowledgments

No leader is complete without the efforts of those skills around them. In the up and down process that is this book, I'd like to thank those who've LIFTed me up:

Mike Henry, Sr. of Lead Change Group. Thank you for giving me a voice in the leadership community and connecting me with other great leaders.

Chery Gegelman and Mary Schaefer, also of Lead Change Group. The two of you are leadership sisters to me. I appreciate your overview of my drafts and correcting and supporting me all the way.

Brandon Johnson, your critical thinking and encouragement mean a great deal to me, brother. Thanks for that boost the last few steps in this process.

My wife, Jennittia. As the heart of our family, you inspire me to do more to LIFT you up.

Thank you LORD, who has LIFTed me up countless times in my life when I've fallen down.

Table of Contents

FOREWARD

What Is Leadership LIFT?

A number of months ago I was reflecting about the profession of a couple of very close friends of mine. They are professional pilots for a private charter line. One day as I was thinking about their fight routines it occurred to me the process of getting a plane off the ground is somewhat similar to lifting a team or company upwards, towards their overall mission.

Great leaders get teams and organizations airborne, lifting them up and sailing forward towards their goals.

Whether you are brand new to leadership, are a successful executive and have seen a great deal of success, or you find yourself in a bit of a rut, all leaders need to acquire LIFT on a regular basis.

LIFT builds influence, develops trust, attains goals, and secures credibility. It changes your direction, moves people and organizations along, and gives you a new perspective on where you are. LIFT also gives leaders the ability to build up others, change the shape of industries, and "boldly go where no one has gone before".

While there are certain physical aerodynamics to take into account for a plane, there are also leadership and organizational "aerodynamics" that come into play as well. Knowing these properties and how to use them can greatly increase the amount of "LIFT" your leadership can give to your teams.

Over the course of this book we'll review how to achieve "Leadership LIFT". Here's a brief outline of our "flight plan":

- Start on the Ground
- Chart Your Course
- Have a Clear Vision
- Sell Tickets
- Get Your People On Board
- Fuel Up
- Check Your Systems
- Throttle Forward and Gain Momentum
- Spread Your Wings
- Adjust Your Altitude and Enjoy the View

Think about these questions and what they mean in your leadership trajectory:

- Where are you leading others?
- Who's on your flight crew?
- Have you gotten off the ground yet?
- How do you keep aloft once in flight?
- Why are you leading to begin with?
- How do you book passengers, customers?

There are many more thoughts that you'll have while you read this book. So I encourage you to use the "NOTES" section at the end of each chapter to write down that thought, resources, plans of action, or inspirational ideas that comes to your mind.

Allow this book to become a resource, a flight manual in which the course is plotted, changed, and mapped out as you go on. Read it, and refer to it often, as well as the other great resources listed at the end.

I look forward to flying with you!! Let's get take off!!

INTRODUCTION

Leadership LIFT:
Take Your Leadership To New Heights

There is a time in all of our professional lives where we need a LIFT - a shot in the arm - to get ourselves and our people to the next level, the next goal.

Everyone, myself included, has periods in our careers where we want to reach new heights in our ability to lead and grow.

We all want to avoid the "Peter Principle" and exceed our "Leadership Lid" as John Maxwell describes. In order to do so, we must take a fresh look at where we are, where we're headed, and how we get there.

If you are at a similar stage as one of these, then this book is geared for you:

- You are about to get ready for a new mission in your professional life.

- You may be starting out in leadership for the first time and need to know how to hit the ground running and make a positive impact.

- You're a seasoned leader who has achieved a great deal of success and are looking to get a shot in the arm to recapture that spark or that edge you once had.

- You may be somewhere in the middle where you've had some success and some failure – perhaps you're even coming off a failure as this moment, and you want to know how to get better at leading.

- You are going through the motions and need to get a second wind into your career.

If this is where you are right now, then this book is for you. My goal here is to provide you with fundamental principles to help you reach that new leadership vista you want to get to.

1

Start on the Ground

We've started the process about giving "LIFT" to your leadership. At every juncture of your leadership trajectory, you need some "LIFT" to go forward, fly farther, and attain new heights.

Let's begin at the most basic point – **starting on the ground.**

One thing that all planes have in common is that they need a place to get readied and embark from - a hangar.

A hangar is designed to hold an airplane or spacecraft in protective storage. Besides protecting the craft from the weather and direct sunlight, it is a place for maintenance and repairs, manufacture, assembly, and storage of the plane as well.

Your hangar will be the things, people, or roles you have that keep you grounded.

For instance, your family may be a source of grounding for you in that they are what drives you and brings purpose to your life. For others, it may be volunteer projects, hobbies, social circles, or community development that gives one a starting point in their life's mission. Company and organizational values also serve as a strong force to keep one grounded in what is important.

Too often leaders don't return to their "hangar" and fail to stay grounded. You don't have to go far, unfortunately, to see examples of men and women forgetting where they came from, who helped them, and losing sight of the big picture in self-destructive pursuits.

Find yourself a "hangar" and stay grounded. Your hangar can be one or many things, but it is crucial that you have a place to embark from, such as:

- Your family.

- Your faith.

- Your home.

- Your organization's vision, mission, core values.

- Your mentor, accountability partners, or anyone or anything that help you keep perspective and stay true to your core values.

- The thrill of helping others grow and have purpose in their lives.

- Financial security for your family.

When a plane is in the hangar it is "grounded." While grounded a plane may be in the process of being repaired. It may allow the crew to rest or be readied for the next flight. An aircraft that does not pull into the hangar to make sure it's worthy of flight will have a high probability of problems on its next mission.

Grounding yourself gives you the following advantages in your leadership prowess. It gives you:

- A place to stop and take a break.

- A chance to refocus on your mission.

- An opportunity to ensure the integrity of your vehicle, which in this case is yourself.

- The chance to reassess your trajectory, and map out new horizons.

- Time to tune-up, refuel, and re-calibrate your internal engines.

How do some of the most influential leaders keep themselves grounded and in touch with those around them? You've seen time and again many leaders that get full of themselves and gradually drift away from reality, credibility, and effectiveness.

Here are some ways that various leaders have stayed rooted in those values that have gotten them to where they are:

- A retail businessman who owned very little outward display of wealth. Drive an old pick-up truck. He lived in a modest house. When visiting his stores, he would open up a cash register to help a store with long lines. – Sam Walton, founder of Wal-Mart

- Two brothers who owned a software company made incredible profits one year, and shared with their entire staff. Over 100 people received bonuses in excess of $100,000 each. They credited their employees as the reason for their success. – Orange County, California

- An early business tycoon who focused on grooming others and looking for the gold in people, rather than the dirt. – Andrew Carnegie

- A young law student who relies heavily on her mentor while going through Harvard and sitting in on courtroom cases. Her mentor informs her that doing well should go hand in hand with her career goals. – Cambridge, Massachusetts

As leaders, you need to be grounded in order to be ready for your continuing mission.

First, you need a starting point. You may be starting from an organization that is breaking down systematically and needs repairs. You may need to get in and remedy these so all systems are go. Perhaps you are just assuming your leadership role and need to get grounded before you start your first flight mission.

Maybe you need a recharging time. Say you've just accomplished a mission and are

21

awaiting your next flight instructions. You may be training to hone your skills and be even more proficient in your duties. As you get ready for the next adventure, you retool and refocus your energies.

This type of grounding is great for the physical aspect of your teams and yourself, but there is another and possibly more important facet of being grounded.

And that is to make sure **you're grounded**.

This is not in a "never-get-off-the-ground" sense, but in the core purpose of why we lead and how we lead. Sometimes leaders get their heads in the clouds and lose sight of reality down below, or get so puffed up and think they can do solo missions from this point on.

As a leader, take those few moments regularly to ensure you stay grounded. Ask yourself:

- **Why am I a leader?**
- **Who am I as a leader?**

- Why do I want to influence others for the better?
- What is my motivation and my higher purpose?
- Where am I truly going?
- Who am I taking along with me?

When you realize that you have a crew, and passengers – customers and/or clients – –who rely on you to get them to their destination safely, you can confidently lead with the peace and assurance that you can, as famous DJ Casey Kasem used to say, "Keep your feet on the ground and keep reaching for the stars."

Stay grounded inside, but LIFT off everywhere else!

KEY THOUGHTS:

NOTES:

2

Chart Your Course

Any time you plan a trip, you will most likely use a map of some type. Whether you're driving, going by train or boat, you will use a map or GPS of your city, scenic areas, or even your hotel. Taxi and bus drivers use maps. They memorize them to more efficiently navigate their routes around town.

Pilots are no different. They need maps of runways, airports, topography, and weather maps to accurately chart their course before flying. They must be able to anticipate any conditions in order to make it to their destination safely and quickly, with no incidents if possible.

Though leaders are the ones who guide and direct the destination of their teams, it would be foolish to rush forward without taking the time to chart your course. A mission towards loftier goals and new heights will never fully be realized unless you take the time to set a course and look at the progress as the journey unfolds.

Even the most experienced leader needs to stop and survey the landscape every so often. Sometimes you can get so mired in the current mission that you miss some of the important landmarks that measures your progress. LIFT yourself out of the trenches, albeit momentarily, in order to get a better view of the landscape ahead and adjust for a better and more successful course.

It was World War I when the fast evolution of the airplane - which was invented just 11 years earlier by the Wright Brothers -

enabled armies to study the battlefield and gain an advantage over the conditions they faced. Just like those brave bi-plane pilots, as a leader, you need to elevate yourself above the circumstances in order to survey the landscape and make more effective maneuvers.

Ask yourself:

- How does our current course compare to our competitors' movement in the industry?

- Are there minefields to avoid? Any potential hazards that we cannot see in our normal pace?

- Or, are there greener pastures ahead for the taking that no one else is noticing?

- Is our crew engaged and seeing the same vision? Do we need to give them a boost to see the scope of vision that we see?

- Am I seeing the entire picture for my team or just the peaks without the pitfalls?

Mark Miller and Ken Blanchard in their book *The Secret – What Great Leaders Know And Do* highlight the "Heads Up, Heads Down" approach to leading. The "heads up" portion is the time of planning, charting your course, and seeing the future.

A great pilot, and a great leader, will take the necessary time to stop and see the future landscape and plan the flight path accordingly.

Stopping to LIFT yourself and your team's vision out of your current circumstances will help you gain a better perspective on where your mission will eventually take you. Don't hesitate to give your team the scope and show them the map. Talk up the mission. As you will see later, your "crew" will be more on board with you as they realize their destination.

Take time to rise above the battlefield and see the big picture of where you're leading. Having a "bird's eye view" of the landscape in which your influence will help you see what is coming and plan accordingly.

Chapter 2 – Chart Your Course

KEY THOUGHTS:

NOTES:

3

Clear the Runway

So far you have grounded
yourself and charted your course to give
more LIFT to your leadership influence.
Now you need to clear the runway.

A great leader will invariably remove all
impediments and barriers to ensure their
teams get off the ground and flying forward.
Any obstacles that a leader doesn't remove
from their organization's mission could
certainly send them off course or crashing
even before they get the project off the
ground.

Having a clear runway in the leadership realm is a combination of having clear vision, clear communication, and removing the obstacles to getting our mission of the ground.

Clear the Runway of Obstacles. Icy patches have caused many aircraft to slide off the runway. Potholes and uneven tarmac will affect the landing gear and cause breakdowns. Even flocks of birds have been known to ground flights until they are cleared. (Some bird flocks have even caused planes to crash down.)

What are the obstacles you need to clear away for your team to move forward? Are there any that you yourself have put in the path that will obstruct the mission? Are there disruptive winds that will give turbulence before takeoff? You will need to clear the way for others to follow.

Make Clear the Journey's Mission to All. Once a man was routed to the wrong destination because he stayed on the plane that he thought was going to "Oakland"

(California). It wasn't until he was over the Pacific and overheard other passengers, that he discovered he was on the "Auckland" (New Zealand) flight. True story!

Does your team have clarity of mission necessary for you to take flight? How can you better present the final destination to your teams to ensure everyone knows where you're leading them?

Are you creating an environment where team members aren't afraid to question the path, to make sure they know the flight they're on, and that others are on board as well? Clear communication will provide this as well.

Have A Clear Vision of What's Ahead. Planes have sophisticated instruments and air traffic controllers to ensure the pilots know what lies ahead and that the flight is a "go", even in the poorest of visibility conditions, they can then confidently take off on their journey. While you may or may not have the outside support or technology needs to see ahead (project plans, capital budgets, mentorships), the one thing all great leaders must possess and instill is a clear vision. As mentioned in *The Secret*, you must "See the Future," even if the landscape is murky.

Uncertain times may be ahead, yet having a perfect scope and confidence of where you are going will engage your staff and make them trust you until the sunny skies shine above.

How can you better clear your path, your communication, and your vision and "LIFT" your leadership influence to the next vista?

Chapter 3 – Clear the Runway

KET THOUGHTS:

NOTES:

4

Sell Tickets

A pilot's purpose is to get their passengers, cargo, and crew to their destination. While the passengers are the paying customers, the flight would not be financially successful unless people paid to come aboard. And people will not fly your airline unless they know you exist.

How does anyone know what new vista you're taking people, what service you're providing, or the exciting adventure that's happening unless you tell people? How do airlines get people to know about their brand, their services, and their routes?

Simple. They advertise and promote their brand. They generate a buzz of who they are and what they do. As a result, they sell tickets.

Southwest Airlines has become a major player in the airline industry not just because of their business model, but also due to their marketing. When you see their commercials, wait at their gate, or board their planes you have a built up expectation of a unique and pleasant experience that you wouldn't find in their competitors.

Their brand, their differentiation, their vision of who they are has influenced you to buy a ticket and travel on their brand.

As a leader you cannot lead alone, you must promote what you represent. Whether it's a brand, mission, project, or steadfast principles, you must advertise and sell others on your vision.

Airlines cannot be profitable having only a few passengers on board. They need to fill their planes and generate as much business on each flight that they can.

The more tickets they sell, the more buzz they promote, the more customers they reach. The more customers are served and satisfied, the more they will help sell the brand. This leverages your efforts and creates a buzz that sells more tickets than you would otherwise.

Business is always about promotion. When you stop selling your mission, your brand, your purpose, you stop growing, individually and corporately.

You need to be selling tickets – all the time.

Chapter 4 – Sell Tickets

KEY THOUGHTS:

NOTES:

5

Get Your People On Board

"He who thinks he leads, but has no followers, is only taking a walk." – Proverb

I don't know who the original writer of that truth was, but I'm positive they were able to LIFT their leadership influence to great heights. Great leaders can only lead and take flight when people are willing to follow.

You've sold the ticket of vision to others so they will understand your message and support you. Now you need to look at the next step in bringing your influence upwards – getting people on board.

There have been countless stories of people who bail out just prior to taking their very first flight. They bought the ticket, but why didn't they get on board for the ride?

The answer is simple – they just didn't have enough trust in either the people or the vehicle to get them to their destination.

Do you know what you call a pilot who only flies himself anywhere, without any passengers? A tourist. In order for a pilot to not just enjoy the sights, but to lead people to a destination, he or she must be able to get people on board their plane.

Whether it's a crew (which we'll discuss in the next section) or passengers, you will need to have people who trust in your ability to get them to where they want to go.

For people to board a particular flight there must be a congruency between both their needs and yours.

There must be a desire to go with you to your envisioned destination. It would be foolish to assume that passengers going to a tropical vacation would take Iceland Air. In the same vein, you cannot expect people to be led if you are going in another direction, or going in no direction. Effective leaders are able to promote a vision that people will want to be a part of, saying to themselves "I want to be there too!!"

There must a trust in your ability to lead them. Leadership without vision will perish and evaporate. Leadership without respect will just spin its wheels and go nowhere. Passengers must inherently give trust to the pilot in order to have faith to get on the plane. Measure your trust factor among your people. Do they have confidence in your ability to pilot them to your destination? Do they trust your knowledge of how to navigate the skies and land safely?

There needs to be a comfort level with the vehicle and systems that you will use. There always tends to be a downturn in flights when a particular airline or type of plane crashes. It takes time before the general population will fly that line or model comfortably again. Ask similar questions like these to determine if your vehicle is worthy of trust in your passengers:

- Is the vehicle (business model, strategy, core values) you're driving sound enough to make it through the turbulence?

- Do your systems check out? Are they sound?

- Have they been run through? Even if there is a glitch, can you correct it in a timely and proper manner that will not adversely affect others? Once on board, your people want to be assured of smooth sailing ahead.

"Passengers" – customers and clients - need to be willing to have you and your team take the controls. They must be willing to allow you to grab the controls and engage the engines. While a great leader will give authority and responsibility away, they also build a large amount of trust that allows other to give some of that back to lead and steer the right course.

Are your people on board, fully engaged? Are your customers or clients on board, loyal to your mission and brand? Build that trust and loyalty through your vehicle, and most importantly, yourself. Your impact is only as good as how well you get others on board.

Chapter 5 – Get Your People On Board

KEY THOUGHTS:

NOTES:

6

Fuel UP

A commercial plane needs jet fuel in order
to go somewhere. Without fuel, the
engine cannot spark and turn over.
There is no energy. There is no
movement.

If there is no fuel in your leadership vehicle,
there is no power, no spark being
generated. You stay still rather than
advance towards your destination.

Fuel, like food, provides energy for our
vehicle to generate momentum. And
whether it's food · or goals, or vision, or
value, or trust – the right fuel is

essential for making any kind of progress.

Identify who needs fuel. Business is all about people, so it's people that need fuel. But which people?

- Your "crew," i.e. your team. They'll need the energy and spark of vision to shoulder the burden with you.

- Your company or organization -- the "control tower". Your boss, executive team, and maybe even trustees or shareholders will need to be fueled up and energized about the prospect of where your efforts and flight path will take them.

- Your "passengers" - your customers. Part of "selling tickets" is building a spark in your audience to get them excited about joining you in your destination.

- And finally, yourself. If you, of all people, don't get the right kind of fuel to create energy and momentum, you cannot expect others to climb on board with you.

Now that you have identified who, needs fuel, we have to figure out what type of fuel is the right kind.

Did you realize that not everyone will have the same level of excitement or benefits from achieving a common goal?

Your people have a variety of motivations for being part of your crew, including: Experience that builds their resume. Skills that are learned. A sense of being part of something greater. Being valued for input. Being part of a team. Opportunity to show their talents. Chances for being in line for a promotion.

Those you report to -"the control tower" - have their own motivations too: Return on investment. Projects done on time. Deadlines met. Being in line with budget. Increased market share. High quality product or service. Little or no wasted resources. No accidents. Good publicity and high chance for repeat customers.

Your customers or passengers have their own intentions too: Getting to their planned destination. No hassles or layovers. Attentive service. Great atmosphere. Arriving safely. Comfortable flight. Product as delivered. Timeliness of the entire route.

Yourself. That, frankly, is up to you and you alone. These are the items we identified in Chapter 1 "Starting On The Ground", where your realized what those values in your "hangar" were that kept your perspective grounded.

Part of your fuel will be what grounds you, what you go to your hangar for. But the other fuel is what gets you going and keeps you going once you've left the hangar, and even become airborne.

But you also need to give your fuel additives to be effective. Consider these items to augment and give your purpose a higher energy content:

Goals. Identify all of your goals. Write them down and post them up. Talk about them, sell them, and promote them. You'll get yourself excited and others around you will help keep that energy flowing as well.

Motivation. Be around people and events that LIFT you up, whether it's spending time with close friends, participating at your church or place of worship, or with hobbies. Maybe you are motivated by listening to other leaders' speeches. The bottom line is that you need to spark some motivation consistently into your days.

Physical Health. This is so often neglected in today's world. We need to fuel our bodies with good food, exercise, and rest, in order to keep running. Balance is the key. An indulgence as a reward is fine; a steady diet of them will bog you down. In everything, moderation is key.

Mental Cessation. We tend to scoff at leisure activities as either frivolous, or we focus too much on them. But a regular period of mental rest will help the brain relax and re-energize itself. (For me it's one night per week.) Reading, gardening, leisure sports, board games, watching a movie, or people watching at the park are great ways to do this. Find an enjoyable yet mentally relaxing activity to do and ensure that you allow some "down time" for your mind.

Input you allow into your mind. Discern what you allow yourself to read, listen to, and watch. If you put low-grade fuel into your tank, the engine won't perform as well. Look for things with substance; sugar will ruin a tank and engine.

Mentors. Seek people of character and credibility to help inspire you and give you valuable insight in your trajectory. Have them hold you accountable, but also ensure that they are invited to your hangar to see what grounds you and how you tune yourself up.

Keep re-fueling. A full tank will only get the plane so far. Then it needs to be refueled. On long missions, military planes refuel in mid-flight, keeping the course going without any interruptions. What can you do during your busy days to keep yourself, your teams, and your passengers fueled without extra pit stops that prolong the goal?

Find the specific type of fuel that best suited for you. Every leader has a different mix that will work for them. If you run on premium, don't put diesel in your tank. If you know you run best by doing certain things in a certain way, don't alter the formula. Use what works for you.

(Side note: There is a coffee blend called "Jet Fuel," which is a very good way to give LIFT to your day!)

Chapter 6 – Fuel Up

KEY THOUGHTS:

NOTES:

7

Check Your Systems

While people are the major resource necessary to accomplish a mission, unless the proper vehicle is utilized your team may find itself stalled out or broken down.

Now you'll need to check your systems, your instrumentation — your gyroscope.

Like an airplane, a vehicle is the means or instrument to get people from one point to another. In the leadership realm, this can take many different forms. Some of the more common vehicles are:

- Business model
- Core Values
- Products made and sold
- Services rendered
- Mission
- Philanthropy
- Company identity or culture

Within these, a leader must verify constantly to ensure that the vehicle's systems are checked, double-checked, and all is "Go". If there is a breakdown of systems, then the flight will be grounded, or even crash. A keen leader will ensure that all systems are aligned and congruent with the team's mission.

Systems vary greatly within each organization and each industry. However, there are some common systems which each organization generally has:

- Hiring systems

- Training systems

- Operational procedures (standard operating procedures)

- Policies – HR, behavioral, cultural, and so forth

- Technical procedures

- Marketing parameters

Here are some examples to get you thinking about your systems:

• Are all decisions made according to your core values? Are you including hiring, training, operating, strategic planning, and financial factors in your thinking?

• Is your business model supported strongly to ensure success to all who buy into it? Whether employees, franchisees, shareholders or customers, is there integrity of the brand to instill confidence and mutual benefit to all?

• Do your products reflect the overt and implied sales pitch your marketing team promotes? Does your team embody the service or product quality you claim to deliver?

• Is your mission clearly communicated to everyone on a consistent, if not daily, basis? Is it backed by the agendas and behaviors of everyone in the leadership team? Do they walk the talk?

• Are you fully promoting the social responsibility and accountability that is in front of the public?

A plane that does not check its fuel, hydraulics, instrumentation, and weather charts will not make it to its destination. A team or organization that does not look after its internal workings will wind down and come to an abrupt halt.

Run your systems through constantly. Find ways to "crash" your model. Figure out ways to tweak these systems to be self-working mechanisms that enhance your flight path. By doing this, you can find ways to improve and ensure your destination is consistently achieved.

Chapter 7 – Check Your Systems

KEY THOUGHTS:

NOTES:

8

Throttle Forward & Gain Momentum

We live in an age of uncertainty. Leaders
fail, markets crash, political agendas
are spun, and material things break down.
It's extremely easy to become a paralyzed at
uncertainty and stay put while the world
bears down on you and runs you over.

Our culture today can also foster the
"paralysis of analysis" syndrome. This is
where you are so overwhelmed with
information and wanting to make so certain
of the next move, that you do nothing.

People today more than ever want to follow leaders that are going somewhere. They don't want to sit on the tarmac, waiting for their flight to taxi. They want their leaders to be people going forward, moving, making things happen.

So, dear leader, what are you waiting for? You've gotten your grounding, have your course charted with a clear vision, people are on board and all systems are "Go!"

Now you need to get moving. You need to _**gain momentum**_.

There comes a time where planning needs to cease, discussions need to wane, and action needs to commence. You need to move the throttle forward and engage the engines. Otherwise, you'll never generate the necessary speed to create wind movement that will LIFT your team off the ground. You cannot allow fear, caution, and second-guessing to be in the co-pilot's position. It has no place in your seat either.

What is holding you back from moving the joystick forward? Engage the engines and move down the runway full speed ahead!!

Leaders will enable their teams to check and fix these systems regularly to ensure smooth sailing.

Chapter 8 – Throttle Forward & Gain Momentum

KEY THOUGHTS:

NOTES:

9

Spread Your Wings

Wings are designed specifically to give LIFT. Air flow on the top moves faster than on the bottom, reducing resistance and allowing the plane to defy gravity with its style, systems, and momentum.

The amount of LIFT is directly related to the amount of surface area of the wings. Without spreading the wings, a plane cannot generate enough LIFT to soar. The bigger and heavier the plane, the more LIFT needed to soar.

In the working world, the same holds true. The bigger the goal, the more LIFT you'll need. The more LIFT needed, the more you'll have to spread your wings to carry your people through.

In order to soar higher, sometimes you need to set that next big, hairy, audacious goal. ("BHAG" from Jim Collins book, *Built To Last)*. Setting the same size goals each time will get similar results, and not propel your company or people much farther than they have already gone.

Think for a moment where these leaders' legacies would be if they hadn't spread their wings to soar to bigger goals:

- **Fred Deluca opening up a second Subway shop when the first one failed and was told by his financial backer to close altogether.**

- **Abraham Lincoln continuing to pursue elected offices even after repeated election defeats.**

- **Soichiro Honda, after being turned down by Toyota for an engineering job, started making motorized scooters, which evolved into developing the Honda Corporation.**

- Rowland Hussey Macy, whose four previous retail stores failed before his namesake store became successful.

- Fred Smith's business idea in his university management class nearly received a failing grade. He persisted with his overnight parcel concept until FedEx came into existence.

As the saying goes, "Goals are in concrete, plans are in sand." These folks and countless others know that if they didn't spread their wings to get more airlift underneath their vision they would crash and fail.

Sometimes a leader must spread their wings and give hope to everyone who is looking to him or her when all seems bleak.

Chapter 9 – Spread Your Wings

KEY THOUGHTS:

NOTES:

10

Adjust Your Altitude and Enjoy the View

There comes a time during every course in your leadership journey to step back and see where you're headed. It's those times that are necessary for you to gauge where you are and to re-orient your crew as to where you are all going.

Up to this point, you've considered many things to give your leadership the running start that's needed:

• Grounded yourself as to who you are and what your mission is.

- Charted a course and mapped to guide you through the turbulence.
- Cleared the runway of obstacles, and your vision now has clarity.
- Promoted your vision and destination and sold everyone a ticket to come aboard.
- Got your people to be on board and trust you.
- Gathered your resources - your fuel – and have found the right mix to keep you and the flight going.
- Proven your vehicle is sound and that all systems are in place.
- Moved forward and gained speed and momentum towards the horizon.
- Spread your wings by stretching farther to attain more wind and more LIFT in order to soar higher and clearer.

Only when you've successfully put the pieces into play and shuttled down the runway can you actually attain that great feeling of flight . . . LIFT.

There is nothing more exhilarating when you're flying than when a plane starts to pull up and separate from the gravitational pull below. Everyone, from pilots to crew to passengers, now know that the journey is underway, and the next stop is your destination, your goal.

Granted, turbulence, weather, and other factors may arise. There will be barriers to overcome. But that is when you trust your crew, your instruments, and your plans to guide you through. Yet, for the most part, the flight is now at its most enjoyable because you'll need to simply adjust your altitude as necessary and enjoy the view.

Your project is implemented and the results are coming in favorable. You've got everyone on board. The systems were checked beforehand. That's how you get that LIFT from using your leadership skills in a new light. And your staff and customers get that LIFT to, in job satisfaction, better quality, improved work culture, and detailed service. Everyone ends up at the destination for different reasons, but your vehicle, and most importantly your leadership style, has taken them there.

There is a tendency in the modern business climate to realize a goal or project deadline and push on to the next goal. There seems to be little time to relish in the journey or the mission. You might even feel guilty to celebrate or enjoy arriving at your destination.

Think about it. Isn't everyone happy when the plane lands at its intended location?

First of all, everyone has arrived safely on the ground. Secondly, the passengers are satisfied that they got what was promised – safe arrival to their desired destination. Lastly, all of the crew get that sense of accomplishment. They met the goal, provided service, and played a role as an integral part of a team.

Being a leader means being the pilot when you're taxiing to the gate. Give the passengers, your customers, a thank you for choosing them. Acknowledge and publicly thank the flight crew, your team.

Depending on the length of the flight and the challenges of the mission, you may want to give extra time to celebrate or acknowledge to your team. Especially with the next mission looming ahead (think connecting flights), a good leader will keep their people motivated and keep the desire to push forward to their next goals strong and fresh.

Leaders, take these steps to give your leadership new LIFT. Get your people to new vistas, destinations where they've never been, and bring people along with you.

Remember, a pilot that has no passengers is just a tourist. Leaders that have no followers, and can't get people to be on board with them, are not leaders at all.

Now it's time to put your flight plan together and give some LIFT to leading!!

Chapter 10 – Adjust Your Altitude & Enjoy the View

KEY THOUGHTS:

NOTES:

EPILOGUE

Applying What You've Read

There are so many techniques and applications of various leadership principles out there. Not every method is right for each leader.

I hope this picture of these leadership principles will at the very least give you some inspiration of picturing how you can LIFT your leadership influence to a new height.

At the most, using the process you've just read will give you a solid framework in which to govern your daily leadership style and help others to LIFT their leadership influence as well.

REMEMBER: Leadership is not about power or position, but about inspiring others to their potential and influencing those around you for a positive impact in your respective world.

So continue to grow and lead. Keep reading, learning, and flying!!!

About The Author

Paul LaRue is a leadership coach, blogger, author, and speaker. His years of senior leadership in many industries – hospitality, retail, entertainment, healthcare, government, and non-profit – have given him tremendous insight as to how best to develop leaders and move organizations forward.

Paul is the creator of The UPwards Leader blog, and a contributing author as an Instigator for the Lead Change Group. His work is also featured on the Leadership series of the Connection Culture website.

Paul lives in central New Hampshire with his wife and children. He is active in his local church ministry. His passions include developing others, reading, golf, board games (cribbage is a must), but mostly seeing leaders grow and positively impact others in their world.

You can follow Paul on these social media:

Twitter: @paul_larue

Google +:
https://www.google.com/+PaulLaRue

Paul's articles are featured on:

The UPwards Leader

http://upwardsleader.com/

Lead Change Group

http://leadchangegroup.com/

Connection Culture

http://connectionculture.com/category/leadership/

Recommended Leadership Books

The Character-Based Leader – Lead Change Group

The Secret – What Great Leaders Know and Do – Ken Blanchard and Mark Miller

Spiritual Leadership – J. Oswald Sanders

Connection Culture – Michael Lee Stallard (with Jason Pankau and Katherine Stallard)

Chess Not Checkers – Mark Miller

Sprinkles – Chip Bell

Energize Your Leadership – Cynthia Bazin, Susan Mazza, Terri Klass, Karin Hurt, Daniel Buhr, Chery Gegelman, Scott Mabry, Jon Metz, and others